A BRAND-NEW WORLD

FAITH-BUILDING STORIES

FOR KIDS

Also by Cari J. Haus:

Learning to Walk With God, with Dwight Hall

To order, call 1-800-765-6955.

Visit us at **www.reviewandherald.com**
for information on other Review and Herald® products.

A BRAND-NEW WORLD

FAITH-BUILDING STORIES

FOR KIDS

CARI HAUS

REVIEW AND HERALD® PUBLISHING ASSOCIATION
HAGERSTOWN, MD 21741-1119

This book was
Edited by Gerald Wheeler
Cover design by Tina Ivany
Cover art by Raoul Vitale
Interior design by Candy Harvey
Electronic makeup by Shirley M. Bolivar
Typeset: 11/13 Cheltenham

PRINTED IN U.S.A.

10 09 08 07 06   5 4 3 2 1

R&H Cataloging Service
Haus, Cari J., 1960-   .
    Faith-building stories for kids. A brand-new world.

    1. Bible stories.   I. Title.

                220.9505

ISBN 978-0-8280-1868-5

Contents

CHAPTER 1

The Most Wonderful Word for God

When you think of a kitten, what comes to your mind? "Kittens are furry," I can almost hear you say. Or "kittens are playful," or "kittens are fun."

If you said any of them, you would be right. Each of these words can describe a kitten.

Of course, we have many other words to describe things as well. For example, we might talk about sparkling water, scorching sun, fluffy clouds, and clear blue sky. There are plenty of ways to speak about people, too. We might call them grumpy, happy, kind, cruel, fearful, courageous, and wise.

Sometimes, when we really want

to tell about something or somebody, one word will shine above all the rest. In fact, it fits perfectly. There is such a word for God.

If you had to pick one word that told all about God—the very best word to describe Him—do you know what that word would be?

Here it is, just in case you haven't already guessed it: God is *love*.

That is the best, biggest, and brightest thing that we could ever say about God. God is love! He cares! And He shows us His love in so many ways, such as:
- Filling the sky with pure fresh air.
- Sending mighty angels to keep us safe.
- Loving us even more than our parents do, and being a Father to us even if something happens to break up our home.
- Designing a beautiful world for us to live in.

Now it's sad to say it, but many people in the world don't understand about God. They don't like Him, don't want to obey Him, and certainly don't think He is love. In fact, some people blame Him for all the bad things that happen in this world. Such as broken bones, sickness, tears, and death.

People who blame God have asked themselves one of the oldest questions in the world: "Whose fault is all this trouble?" And for whatever reason, they choose to answer that question "God."

Of course, if God really is love, He can't also be the one who started bad things. It was Satan who caused this world to be filled with pain.

To understand this, of course, you have to take a little trip. You must go back in time, past when your grandparents and great-grandparents were born.

Back before Abraham Lincoln, Thomas Jefferson, and George Washington. Back before Christopher Columbus, Martin Luther, and all the kings, queens, and princes who ever lived. Back before Jesus, Jezebel, Joshua, and Joseph. You even have to go back before Adam and Eve. And there, thousands of years ago, is just where our story begins—in a beautiful place called "Heaven."

CHAPTER 2

A Perfectly Peaceful Place

It's hard to imagine what heaven must have been like in those days, or even what it's still like today. But we can catch a glimpse of that perfectly peaceful place in the book of Revelation. There John, one of Jesus disciples, watched the holy city, New Jerusalem, coming down out of heaven from God, prepared as a bride dressed up for her husband (Revelation 21:2).

John saw a city filled with the glory of God, dazzling like jasper in the warmth of the morning sunlight. A crystal clear wall surrounds the shining city. It must be a truly impressive sight, for the wall is more than 200 feet high and hundreds of miles in length.

The wall has 12 pearly gates. The number 12 seems to be special in heaven, for the names of the 12 tribes of Israel are each engraved on one of the 12 gates.

The number seven must be special, too, for John speaks about seven spirits before God's throne, seven seals on a special scroll, and seven angels with shiny trumpets.

Heaven has thousands of other angels, too, all ready to help God with His work in the universe. The seraphim, which have six wings, sit high above God's throne. Another kind of angel, the cherubim, have four wings each. Angels carry out God's errands, zipping from planet to planet and even to Earth when needed. They also sing in the heavenly choir the most beautiful music.

High above the walls of heaven, surrounded by a gorgeous greenish rainbow, is a truly magnificent throne. It's the throne of God, Creator of this world, source of all life, and ruler of all the universe. A mighty river of life flows out of His throne and into the holy city.

If you could float on that river (and someday I hope we all will) you would soon look up at the leaves of a massive tree. Called the tree of life, it spans the river of life like a giant, towering bridge. Its fruit is better than a banana split, chocolate swirl, or the best desert you could ever think of, and it comes in 12 scrumptious flavors—one for each month of the year. The leaves of this tree are special, too. They can heal people.

Some think of heaven as a magical pretend place. But it's not that way at all, for unlike Willie Wonka's chocolate factory or the Land of Oz or 1,000 other

make-believe places, heaven is very real. And it's much more special than Sea World, Disneyland, or even a dream vacation.

CHAPTER 3

Trouble in Paradise

It's hard to imagine that anything terrible could ever happen in a place as peaceful and happy as heaven, but the Bible tells us that something incredibly sad did indeed take place there.

It all started with Lucifer, the best and brightest angel God ever made. A guardian cherub, Lucifer's job was to spread his wings over the very throne of God. The prophet Ezekiel tells us that Lucifer was wise and beautiful (Ezekiel 28:12).

In big cities today some people like working in the top of the highest building. From their high vantage point they can see the sights and sounds of the city stretched out beneath them. Well, Lucifer's "office" must have been something like that, next to

God's throne, under the emerald rainbow. No doubt Lucifer had a gorgeous view of the river of life, tree of life, and the pearly gates of the city.

Lucifer must have been a very gifted angel. He was the greatest singer in heaven, because he led the angel choir. But best of all, Lucifer knew God very well. As the angel who stood next to His throne, he couldn't help knowing how kind and gracious and caring God really was. After all, he worked with Him closely every day.

Unfortunately, however, Lucifer began to notice that he was the best and brightest angel in the whole universe.

The prophet Ezekiel said of Lucifer, "Your heart became proud on account of your beauty, and you corrupted your wisdom because of your splendor" (Ezekiel 28:17).

Of course, there was nothing wrong with Lucifer's *being* an incredibly gifted angel. After all, God made him that way so that he could be a leader. And there was even nothing wrong with Lucifer *knowing* he was gifted, for everyone else knew that too.

No, the big mistake Lucifer made was not in being the best or knowing he was the best. The problem was that Lucifer became proud and selfish. He wanted to be king of the universe instead of God. In fact, he wanted to be God!

"I will ascend to heaven," Lucifer said in his heart. "I will raise my throne above the stars of God; I will sit enthroned on the mount of assembly . . . I will make myself like the Most High" (Isaiah 14:13, 14).

Lucifer forgot that no matter how high he was, he was still created by God and Jesus. Making Lucifer as important as God or Jesus would have been just as bad as letting that first airplane be the owner of the Wright brothers! It just couldn't be. But Lucifer didn't care about that. He wanted to rule with or in place of God, and he didn't want anyone—not even Jesus Himself—to get in his way.

It's a sad, sad story, but one that needs to be told: how Lucifer, God's brightest and shiniest angel became the ruler of darkness, turning into the devil.

CHAPTER 4

One Bad,
Tiny Seed

Lucifer didn't fall from his position as God's mightiest angel all at once. In the beginning just a little seed of selfishness sprouted in his mind. But Lucifer watered it. And sometimes, when he was by himself, he would sit and think about how special and important he really was. In the words of the Bible, his heart became lifted up because of his beauty.

After a few months of thinking about how wonderful, handsome, and talented he really was, something else began to fill his thoughts. He now kept thinking about Jesus, God's son. And the more he thought about Him, the more Lucifer hated Him.

Of course, Lucifer didn't start out feeling hate. In the beginning he didn't even know what hate was. It was just a little seed of dislike in his heart. But Lucifer watered his seeds of pride and dislike until they grew into such mighty trees of selfishness that they pushed any love right out.

At first he kept his feelings to himself. Deep inside, he knew that his thoughts were wrong. But pretty soon his feelings became too strong to hide any longer. He began to share them with others.

Lucifer was pretty sneaky about spreading his ideas. He kept sowing his little seeds in the minds of others, saying things here and there, making himself look better and Jesus look bad.

It especially upset him that God and Jesus hadn't asked his advice when they planned the new world they would make. He also didn't like it when God and Jesus spent time by Themselves discussing how things should be done.

God knew what Lucifer was doing all along, of course, and it made Him feel very sad. The Bible tells us that God respects the humble, but He can see pride from a long way off (Psalm 138:6). In fact, of the many sins God hates, pride is number one and telling lies is number two (Proverbs 6:16-19). Sadly enough, Lucifer was specializing in both of these sins.

Although God had the power to squash Lucifer and his selfish ideas right from the start, He didn't. You see, God is a God of love! He really cared about Lucifer. And it deeply saddened Him that the strongest, shiniest, best, and brightest angel He had ever made would turn against Him this way. Especially when God had done absolutely nothing bad, because (and here's

another important thing about Him), He never changes (Malachi 3:6). He has always been "merciful and gracious, longsuffering, and abounding in goodness and truth" (Exodus 34:6, KJV), and He will always be that way. But God didn't just sit around and do nothing about Lucifer's antics, either.

"Come . . . let us reason together" (Isaiah 1:18) is God's message of love to us humans, and He surely must have said the same thing to Lucifer. In other words, God said to him, "Let's get together and talk things through." God wanted Lucifer and all the angels to understand Him and the things He did.

"Lucifer, I love you," He must have said. "I made you, and I want you to be with me."

Even Lucifer had left his job under the emerald rainbow to spread his selfish ideas, God offered to hire him back. His old office, overlooking the river of life, the tree of life, and the pearly gates of the city, was still open. The very thought of having Lucifer back must have set the whole angel choir to singing, for they didn't sound nearly as good without his voice soaring above all the rest.

How God must have smiled at Lucifer, and what a kind, loving, and forgiving smile it must have been.

"Please come back," He whispered in Lucifer's ear. "We all want you here."

Lucifer nodded. He even looked as if he wanted to return. But then the next minute he didn't seem so sure. A terrible struggle was going on in his heart—a battle between right and wrong, good and evil, kindness and selfishness. Along with every angel in heaven God waited for his decision. But Lucifer didn't want to decide—at least not yet.

"I'll think about it," he said. The mightiest angel nodded toward his Creator—and then, turning on his heel, walked away from the emerald rainbow.

CHAPTER 5

Father of Lies

Poor Lucifer! What a terrible struggle raged in his heart. It all made God feel very sorry for him. In fact, God did everything He could to try and win Lucifer back. Everything, that is, except change Himself. For as God has said so clearly in His Holy Word, God doesn't change.

Of course, the heavenly tug-of-war was pretty hard on the angels, too. While they loved Lucifer very much, they also loved God even more.

Though Lucifer teeter-tottered back and forth and changed his mind almost every hour for a while, the wrong finally won. Lucifer made his choice: he would fight the God who had made him!

God could have forced him to obey

right then and there. But as we've said earlier, that's not how He likes to work. Our God is love! So God just told the angels the truth about Himself and let the rebellious angel say what he wished about Him.

It was then that Lucifer learned how to lie. Oh, he had told little half-truths all along. But now he became bolder and bolder in his lies about God.

"God is mean and unfair," he told the angels. "He doesn't care about you the way I do! You need me, Lucifer, to lead you and stand up for you."

The angels were confused. They had never heard anyone tell a lie before, so they just expected to hear the truth. As a result, Lucifer tricked many of them.

For His part, God told the angels that He did love them. He even explained to them how Jesus, who had helped to make Lucifer, was God's very special Son. But, sadly, many of the angels wouldn't listen.

Then God looked down from His beautiful throne and, for the first time in the history of the universe, tears flowed freely in heaven. They were God's tears, mixed with angel tears, as together they cried over what was happening to their city—their beautiful, once-peaceful city.

Because God knows everything, He knew that heaven could never be happy again with Lucifer and his followers there. And though God is "slow to anger, abounding in love and faithfulness, . . . and forgiving wickedness, rebellion, and sin. Yet He does not leave the guilty unpunished" (Exodus 34:6, 7). The time had come to do something about Lucifer and his antics.

Then there was war in heaven (Revelation 12:7-9). Jesus and His angels fought against Lucifer, and Lucifer and his angels fought back. Matching strength against strength, friend against former friend, they fought until Lucifer and every last one of his angels were thrown out of heaven.

Time and again, God had asked him to stay. Again and again Jesus had pleaded with Lucifer's friends. The loyal angels had tried to help, too, working with their friends, trying to win them back. But in the end, Lucifer and his angels made a final and very sad decision.

Lucifer had become Satan, the angel became a dragon, the Son of the Morning had sunk to become the father of lies. It was an incredibly sad day, for when Lucifer finally left, one third of the angel choir's singers went with him. As followers of Satan, they had lost their place in heaven. And together with Satan, they weren't coming back.

CHAPTER 6

Silence in Heaven

It was quiet in heaven for quite a while after Lucifer left. The war was over, but nobody felt like singing. In His throne room God and Jesus shared a good long Father and Son talk. Together, they decided to go ahead with Their plans to make a new world.

We know this, of course, because the Bible tells us that "in the beginning was the Word, and the Word was with God, and the Word was God. He was with God in the beginning. Through him all things were made; without him nothing was made that has been made" (John 1:1-3). So Jesus, or "the Word," worked together with the Father to plan this planet we live on.

It would be a beautiful, happy place—more complicated and special than anything God and Jesus had made before. And in the middle of that beautiful new world God decided to put somebody who, like the world he lived in, would also be very special. He would be a new being—one made in the image of God (Genesis 1:27). Someone God could talk with and sing with and love very dearly.

Someday, if these new family members proved loyal to Him and His kingdom, they could even move up to heaven. God wanted to fill the courts of heaven again—with the happy, loving voices of His children.

Outside the Holy City, Satan and his angels kept watch at the gates of heaven. They knew something big was about to happen, for God still allowed Satan to come to some of heaven's meetings.

We know this because the book of Job tells us of one such day when the angels presented themselves before the Lord, and Satan also came with them (Job 1:6).

When Satan heard God's angels talking about the new world, he couldn't have been more interested. You see, he was looking for a new place to live himself. It turns out that life in outer space was rather chilly, especially compared to the warmth and light of heaven.

How nice of God to create a "little heaven on earth," Satan must have thought in his own sarcastic way. *I wonder if I can get it away from Him.*

As Lucifer, Satan had brought such sadness to heaven. Now he wanted to do the same on the new world. And so while God and the Father finished planning this planet, Satan was also busy—figuring how he could wreck it.

CHAPTER 7

Light in the Darkness

Have you ever been in a place so dark you couldn't see your hand if you stuck it one inch from your nose? Have you ever been somewhere so cold that you felt chilled to the very insides of your bones? And have you ever been in a place so wet and watery there was no way you could ever get dry? Well, that's exactly how our world was thousands of years ago.

Yes, if you put those three words together—dark, cold, and wet—that's exactly the way it was. Because there was no light there were no orchids or ostriches on our planet. Because there was no air, there were no kangeroos or cougars or kittens. And because there was no land, there were no trilliums, trees, or trails. Instead there was just one vast, cold, and incredibly dark ocean of blackness—stretching for miles and miles across the surface of our world.

And it was this place—this unpromising, miserable blob of nothingness—that God chose to transform into the crown jewel of all His creation.

"Why did He do it?" you say. "Why didn't He choose a place that at least had more things that He could have worked with?"

Well, if you step from one gorgeous garden into another, it's not that big of a deal. But if you come from an arid desert into the greenery of a luscious oasis, there's an incredible difference. Or if you walk from the depths of a cave into the glory of sunlight, the view is truly wonderful. There's quite a change between the eye of a vicious storm and the peaceful sunset that follows. And there was no comparison between the way the earth was *before* and *after* Creation.

God probably wanted it that way, for it just made the new world all the more spectacular. The Bible tells us that on that spectacular first day of creation "the earth was formless and empty, darkness was over the surface of the deep, and the Spirit of God was hovering over the waters" (Genesis 1:2).

The Bible also says that "God is light; in Him there is no darkness at all (1 John 1:5). That explains why God did what He did almost as soon as He arrived at our planet as it spun through space.

"And God said, 'Let there be light,' and there was light" (Genesis 1:3). Maybe a soft glow began to creep over the horizon, growing brighter with each passing moment until the whole watery mess was awash in a

blaze of glory. Perhaps God put on a spectacular show of heavenly fireworks. Or maybe He just threw the switch, lighting this planet with one fell swoop. You know, like your parents (or brother or sister) flip the switch in your bedroom and light up your world when your eyes are still stuck shut from sleep.

However it was, we can learn much about God from what He did on the very first day of Creation. He is light and love, warmth and gladness, power and glory all wrapped up in one magnificent, holy Being. And He brings those very same attributes with Him wherever He goes.

This world could never stay dark when God was here for "He wraps himself in light as with a garment" (Psalm 104:2), "He knows what lies in darkness, and light dwells with him" (Daniel 2:22). His very presence warmed the coldest planet, created something out of nothing, and lit up the landscape for thousands and thousands of miles.

Of course, if God can do such things on this earth, just think what He can do in your heart. Even if you're feeling cold, clammy, and dark, God can warm your insides and give you a happy glow all over, for "the path of the righteous is like the first gleam of dawn, shining ever brighter till the full light of day" (Proverbs 4:18).

CHAPTER 8

Each in Its Order

If you've ever watched builders working on a house, you know they must do things in a certain order. First they have to put in a foundation to support and hold up the house. Then come floor joists, walls, and a roof.

It would never work to skip a step. If you built a roof only, what would you set it on? Or if you skipped the foundation, your walls might crumble and fall. Jesus Himself spoke of "a foolish man who built his house on sand. The rain came down, the streams rose, and the wind blew and beat against that house, and it fell with a great crash" (Matthew 7:26, 27).

Yes, there's a right way to construct

a house, and the builder must think things through before he or she even starts it.

No doubt God understood all this when He built the world, for He did everything in the right order. It would have been fun to make puppies and kittens on the very first day, but what would they have breathed? Where would their parents find food? There wasn't even one mound of dirt for a puppy to dig a hole in!

In order to create this world as He did, our God had to be more than a great builder. He had to be a great scientist and mathematician too. God also had to have everything figured out in advance—otherwise, life couldn't have existed on our planet.

Fortunately, God had things worked out very well. "Turning on the lights" for our dark planet had warmed things up quite a bit. But now God wanted to make things even more pleasant. He needed air, otherwise known as atmosphere, for His lions and leopards to breathe. Great blue herons would need air to fly in, and even greenery—from the towering redwoods to the tiniest tulip—would have to have air to survive.

It would have to be just the right kind of air, too. So God mixed up some gases called oxygen and nitrogen—just in the right amounts. The earth would wear this atmosphere as it hurtled through space. It would protect the humans and hyacinths and hippos from the burning rays of the sun.

In the beautiful words of the book of Job:

> "He spreads out the northern [skies] over
>   empty space;
> he suspends the earth over nothing.

He wraps up the waters in his clouds,
> yet the clouds do not burst . . .
He marks out the horizon on the face of the
> waters for a boundary between light and
> darkness.
The pillars of the heavens quake,
> aghast at his rebuke.
By his power he churned up the sea . . .
By his breath the skies became fair . . .
And these are but the outer fringe of his works;
> how faint the whisper we hear of him!
Who then can understand the thunder of his
> power?" (Job 26:7-14).

As He turned out the lights at the end of day two, God smiled at the work He had done. Perhaps He was thinking of the eels and elephants, pandas, ponies, and polar bears He would create very soon. Or maybe He thought of the humans who would draw this fine air in and out of their lungs for centuries on end.

Although we don't know just what thoughts went through God's mind on that day, we do know He was very pleased with His work. Another evening and morning had passed, day two of creation was over, and so God turned out the lights.

CHAPTER 9

God "Wraps" the World

Back when God made the world, the weather reports weren't quite as exciting as they are today. No doubt the forecasts for Wednesday, Thursday, and Friday were all the same: "Sunny and warm, sunny and warm, sunny and warm." The cushion of air around our planet helped to keep the temperature comfortable and make things pleasant and peaceful.

Although God had already accomplished much in His great plan for this world, He still had much more to do. He could have made us humans to be life-long swimmers like dolphins or whales or fish, but God wanted to give us something more solid to set our feet on. It wasn't quicksand or mud He was looking for here, for they would have been too soft. Nor did He want rocks for the crust of the earth either, for then the land would have been too stony and hard.

So God in His great wisdom put the rocks underneath as a framework or foundation for the rich earth He would place above them. Just how God made the land the Bible does not tell us. But we do know that His "hand laid the foundations of the earth" (Isaiah 48:13), and that He "spread out the earth" (Isaiah 44:24) by Himself. The Bible tells us that God said, "Let the water under the sky be gathered to one place, and let dry ground appear" (Genesis 1:9).

Instantly, the peaceful waters began to move. A gentle breeze began to stir, then became stronger and stronger as it whipped into a mighty wind. And it was pushing, pushing at the water all over this world, sweeping it back as if making room for something else.

And there was indeed something else! There was land—lots of it—shuddering and shaking as it rose above the water. Soon the earth had more land than water, as God stirred up mountains of rich black mud, packing them over the rugged foundation of rocks. It would be the perfect soil for pansies, petunias, and pine trees to grow in.

Then, with a sweep of His giant finger, God channeled a path through the dark mud. Perhaps the big grove had a dam at the end of it, to keep water from rushing in while He sprinkled sand on the banks of the soon-to-be-river. Finishing with a flourish of pebbles and rocks for the waters to ripple over, God let in the mighty sea. Then water surged into the channels, obediently following the paths He had made.

For it was God, the great God of the universe, "who shut up the sea behind doors, when it burst forth from the womb" (Job 38:8). It was the great God of the universe who set the boundaries of the sea with bars and doors, saying "This far you may come and no farther; here is where your proud waves halt" (Job 38:8-11).

No doubt God spent quite a bit of time carving out places for rivers and valleys, brooks and the shining sea. But when He was finished, the earth was truly starting to take shape.

Gentle waves lapped at the shore of a large lake. It was ready for bluefish and trout. Pebbles of gold and silver glistened in a babbling brook. They were ready for frogs to hop on. Rows of rolling, majestic hills looked over the whole happy scene. Grounded on rocks and dressed in the richest black dirt, they waited for God to plant grass, gardenias, and grapefruit trees on them.

And now God, the great God of the universe, was ready to cover His gift of a new world with a living "wrapping paper." At that moment this incredible world He was making for people to live, eat, and sleep on was still in its simple, brown-wrapper state. But our God, who delights in designs and textures and color, wasn't about to leave things that way. Like a giant birthday present, He wanted to decorate the world. And so He began to speak again.

"Let the land produce vegetation: seed-bearing plants and trees on the land that bear fruit with seed in it, according to their various kinds" (Genesis 1:11).

Suddenly there came the rustle of rapid growing. Almost immediately, tiny shoots popped up all over the earth, wiggling their way toward the sky. Many of them didn't have far to grow. They were the blades of golden grass that would soon carpet the earth. Others became thicker and stronger as they stretched above the grass. The angels, peering out of the portals of heaven above, no doubt looked on in amazement.

"That must be a bush!" one said.

"No, it's a tree," another declared.

"Will it ever stop growing?" murmured a third as leafy branches jutted higher, higher, and still higher into the sky above.

By now, a gorgeous picture spread under the canopy of the towering redwood trees. Pine trees, birch, and sassafras, which seemed to have sprouted everywhere, reached gracefully up to the sky. Underneath stood a magnificent array of bushes, some green, some yellow, some red—just waiting for a human hand to trim them into some fancy shape or train them into arches and arbors.

Tucked beneath some of them was a vivid array of black-eyed Susans, begonias, and Jack-in-the-pulpits. It was the very first flower arrangement, and oh what a picture it was. This world was getting ready—yes, it was almost ready for the crowning work of creation. But not quite. God still had a few things to do, but they'd have to wait until another day.

And God looked at everything He had made, and behold, it was very good. "And the evening and the morning were the third day" (Genesis 1:13, KJV).

CHAPTER 10

Rulers by Day and Night

During the first three days of creation God may have lit up this once dark planet with His own magnificent glory. And that was certainly no problem for Him, for "God is light, and in him is no darkness at all" (1 John 1:5, KJV). But He had a plan for this planet—a plan that stretched beyond the cushion of blue surrounding its landscape of towering trees and golden-emerald grass.

God had a set of lights to warm and illumine the earth. A series of softer lights would be just right for the night, but He wanted an incredible spotlight, one much bigger, brighter, and warmer for the day.

"And God said, Let there be lights in the

firmament of the heaven to divide the day from the night; and let them be for signs, and for seasons, and for days, and years: and let them be for lights in the firmament of the heaven to give light on the earth: and it was so. And God made two great lights; the greater light to rule the day, and the lesser light to rule the night: he made the stars also" (Genesis 1:14-16, KJV).

Lighting our planet was only one of the jobs the Lord gave to the sun, moon, and stars. In the words of the psalmist, "the moon marks off the seasons . . . the sun knows when to go down" (Psalm 104:19). Together, they would also help humans keep track of days, months, and years. For the earth was spinning, spinning, spinning—just like a giant ball. When your side of the world is turned toward the sun, it's daytime. Then, when the spot where you live moves away from the sun, it's night.

From your one little point on the planet it looks as if the sun climbs up one side of the sky and slides down the other. But it's the world that's really moving, and every time it rotates completely around once, it makes a day.

It's hard to imagine, but this world is also rocketing through space. Its path, or orbit, zings our little planet around the sun one time every year.

If you're seven years old, that means the earth has taken its trip seven times in your lifetime. But if you were Methuselah, you would have rocketed around the sun 969 times (Genesis 5:27)! Of course, it doesn't seem as if we are traveling through space from where we are on our planet. But that's how people have kept track of years for centuries on end: one orbit equals one year.

The moon had a role to play also. The full or "new moon" has helped people keep track of the months as they rolled on by. The gravity of the moon pulls the ocean tides in and out, day after day after day. The tides help bring food to many animals that live along the seacoasts.

God gave us the sun, moon, and stars to help us keep track of time, as well as to brighten our world. They can also teach us many things. In other words, we can learn many beautiful lessons by studying these giant orbs as they hurtle through space, obediently following the paths God set up for them.

Just as the sun lights up the world, God wants to light up our lives. Jesus, as the Sun of Righteousness would appear with "healing in his wings" (Malachi 4:2, KJV). When we bask in the light of God's presence—which means living close to God—our hearts will be softened and warmed. Just as the daffodils turn their faces to the sun every day, we should turn our hearts toward Jesus. Then, and only then, can we grow and live healthy spiritual lives.

The moon can't make light by itself, and neither can we. But we can reflect the light of God, helping others to see through the darkness of sin.

The sun, because of its size, has a great amount of gravity or "pull" that holds our world in its orbit, circling around the sun. And God is like that. He is great and powerful and strong. And there is something attractive about Him, a "pull" that can set our lives in order and keep us in the right path.

The moon, though smaller, also tugs on our world. It influences what happens here. And so do we. The moon could never grip our world like the sun, but it does pull on the water and cause the ocean tides. And we, by setting a good example in our lives, may help hold back the tide of evil in this world. In the beautiful words of Daniel, "those who are wise will shine like the brightness of the heavens, and those who lead many to righteousness, like the stars for ever and ever"(Daniel 12:3).

When we think of these things—when we "consider your heavens, the work of your fingers, the moon and the stars, which you have set in place" (Psalm 8:3), it's easy to ask God, as did the psalmist, "What is man that you are mindful of him, the son of man that you care for him?" (Psalm 8:4).

We are such tiny specks in a vast universe, yet God has loved us so. It should make us all want to sing with the angels:

> "Praise him, sun and moon,
> praise him, all you shining stars.
> Praise him, you highest heavens
> and you waters above the skies.
> Let them praise the name of the Lord,
> for He commanded and they were
> created.
> He set them in place for ever and ever;
> he gave a decree that will never pass
> away" (Psalm 148:3-6).

CHAPTER 11

The End of a "Silent Spring"

Have you ever imagined what it would be like to wake up in a world of total silence? A world that, though totally beautiful, had not one single barking dog, croaking frog, or bog filled with thousands of spring peepers? A world where no robins, redstarts, or rose-breasted grosbeaks ever warbled?

You might think it would be nice not to hear the voice of your mother, brother, or sister for a few days. Or you might not want to hear what your daddy has to say. But, as many who have lost their hearing could tell you, the sound of silence gets old very quickly.

It was a beautiful spring day, that fifth

day of creation. You might have even heard a few sounds that morning. Perhaps water lapping gently on the shores of a lake, bubbling over nuggets of gold in a mountain stream, or pounding at the bottom of a huge waterfall. A gentle breeze probably rustled through the towering trees. But mostly there was silence.

Of course, God intended to change all of that—though not in one day. But He had something special planned for this, the fifth day of creation. He may have started at the bottom—the bottom of a lake. There He formed the very first clownfish, goldfish, and starfish. They didn't make much noise, of course. But God had only begun. When He finished making bluefish, trout, and a thousand other kinds of fishes, He turned His attention to the larger creatures of the deep, such as stingrays, dolphins, and friendly white sharks.

"Balooga!" The very first whale popped his head above the surface and shot a spray of water 50 feet in the air.

"What in the world was that?" In the courts of heaven above some of the angels jumped. Once again they peered through the portals, watching to see what God would make next.

Far below, on the little blue planet called Earth, God sure was keeping busy! The angels stared in fascination at their Creator patting the head of a porpoise and stroking the sides of a seal. Maybe they saw Him smiling, wading next to a walrus, before setting His sights on something much higher up.

"What is He making now?" the tall angel murmured to a little angel. God had something little in His hand, and He was reaching up, up, up to the very tip-top of the tallest tree in the world.

"I—I—I don't know what to call it," the smaller angel stuttered in amazement. "It's tiny, with gorgeous red feathers. Look how it holds itself on a branch with its little yellow feet!"

"It moves!" whispered another angel as the father of all scarlet tanagers stretched and flexed its wings for the very first time.

"It sings!" giggled another, as Papa Tanager warbled his first melodious song.

"Hallelujah! It flies!" shouted the little angel as the tiny tanager sailed into the sky.

"Where is it going?" The angels weren't sure what all the fluttering was about, but one thing seemed certain: Mr. Tanager was very busy. His first official act, of course, was to look for Mrs. Tanager. *That* didn't take long, of course, for she was sitting demurely nearby, just hoping that he would find her. After preening each others feathers and singing a gorgeous duet, the happy couple flew off to look for their first apartment. Well, not quite, but they did have a lot of checking to do before deciding on the perfect tree for their nest, and a lot of songs to sing about the whole operation.

Across the river, just over a mountain on the shores of a sleepy pond, God had just introduced Mr. and Mrs. Flamingo. Then a pair of peacocks strutted forth from His hand. When he was sure Mama Peacock was watching, Papa Peacock spread out his breath-taking, feathery fan.

"Zing!" A ruby-throated hummingbird whizzed past the peacocks and off to find its mate.

"Cock-a-doodle do!" a rooster strutted proudly.

"Balooga!" answered the giant blue whale.

The angels in heaven were amazed. "Did you

ever see such a sight?" they said to each other.

"Did you hear the songs—the wonderful songs—of those feathery, flying friends?" wondered another.

"They make me want to sing too," one angel said.

"Me too," said God's mightiest angel as he lined up the angel choir. It was indeed time for a heavenly song, for like their feathery friends and us humans, singing is how angels show they are happy. And there was much to be happy about on this, the fifth day of creation. The angels were filled with love for God and praise for His holy name. So they sang.

Far below them, a different chorus was also lifting its voice in praise to their heavenly King. The sun had set on planet earth, but the scene was no longer silent.

"Whoo—hoo—hoo!" hooted the great horned owl. The cry of a loon rang over the waters, while a frog croaked from a log in a bog. Although these songs of the night were different, they said much the same thing.

"Praise be to God!"

"Thank You for making us!"

The songs of the crickets and peepers floated up with the song of the angels to the very ears of God. And there on His throne, under the emerald rainbow, God saw everything that He had made, that it was very good. "And the evening and the morning were the fifth day" (Genesis 1:23, KJV).

CHAPTER 12

The Very First Llamas and Lions

When the sun crept into the sky at the start of day six, the rivers, lakes, and sky above them were fairly bursting with life. Bluefish and salmon swam happily in little pools while minnows darted merrily here and there. A pair of ostriches ambled through a meadow, a grouse drummed his feathers somewhere deep in the forest, and an eagle soared high in the sky.

But though the water and sky above it were fairly bursting with life, the land below was mostly empty of creatures. In other words, the earth had no monkeys to swing from a branch, no hippos to dip in a pool, no lions to roar, and not one single pony to ride.

Of course, God planned to change all of this. He had a lot of work ahead of Him at the start of day six.

"Wow!" the angels exclaimed from the portals above as they watched the parade of animal pairs marching out of God's earthly workshop.

Maybe God started with the smaller creations, such as hamsters and bunnies and gerbils. Then He moved on to the larger animals. When God put a mask on the face of Father Raccoon, or humps on the back of the very first camel, or a mane on the neck of Father Lion, how the angels must have chuckled. And they would have laughed even harder if they could have seen the parade of playful puppies, capering colts, and frisky young foxes that would very soon burst on the scene. But God wasn't making baby bears this day. He would leave that up to Mama and Papa Grizzly. Nor did He make puppies either. He just prepared it so Daddy Dog and his furry wife could and would plan a fun little family of their own.

As day six wore on, life on Planet Earth grew more and more exciting. Perhaps the angels even spilled out of heaven to help, since there were so many new couples to introduce to each other. It's hard to imagine just what it would have been like. No doubt there was a whole lot of snorting, nose touching, and nuzzling going on.

Of course, once they got acquainted with their mates, all the animals had to get used to each other.

"What in the world are you!" Grandfather Giraffe must have thought as he stretched his neck down, down, and still farther down to examine a happy hippo.

"My, but you have a long neck!" bellowed the hippo as he craned his own short little neck up, up

and still farther up to peer at the friendly giraffe.

"Could I drink from your pool of water?"

"Please pardon my tail!" and

"Why do you have two humps?" are just some of the things that may have been said, through bellows and barks and grunts, during those very first moments of creature creation.

No doubt God had a lot of fun walking among the animals, petting the ponies, shaking the paw of a dignified dalmatian, and cuddling the first woolly sheep.

The animals were still getting acquainted when God headed down toward the sandy banks of a river. The kangeroos and cats might not have noticed when He stopped His work and stood quietly on the sand with a very thoughtful look on His face. But the angels did. They might not have known the details, but they guessed that God had something very important yet to make. Something—someone—so much different than the animals. Someone more intelligent, more noble and kingly than anything He had yet put on earth. Someone God could love, talk with, and be a friend to.

Kneeling down in the sand, God began His work. First He moistened His giant hands in the cool, fresh water. Next He started to shape some of the soil along the bank. The Bible doesn't tell us where God started first. He might have started with a handsome nose, or He might have begun with some very large toes. But we do know that sometime on the sixth day of creation, God knelt over the sculpture of a massive, incredibly fine-looking masterpiece of artistic design. And that within seconds that person would be Adam, the friend and son of God—Adam, the very first human being.

CHAPTER 13

Crown of Creation

God could have brought Adam to life with a snap of His mighty fingers. Or He could have spoken Him into existence with a simple "Wake up!"

But that's not how God chose to finish this, His crowning work of creation. He wanted to do something up close and personal, for this would be His new child. And so God leaned over the perfectly formed mud-man. Placing His elbows on the sand, He cradled the man's head in His own giant hands and "breathed into his nostrils the breath of life" (Genesis 2:7).

Instantly a current of energy surged through the silent sculpture. The moist soil morphed into skin and bones, fingernails, eyebrows and eyelashes. Inside the man now had muscles to move him, a stomach to feed him, a brain to guide him, and a heart to pump life through it all.

With a flutter of eyelashes the man opened his eyes for the very first time. The massive chest heaved upward; the finely shaped mouth drew in its very first breath. The man twitched a finger, then a toe, just to see if they worked. Then he blinked and focused his eyes. And the very first thing he saw was the wonderful eyes of God. For God was still there, just inches away from his face.

The Lord smiled into the man's eyes, and the man smiled back. Next He squeezed the man's hand, and the man squeezed back. When God sat up, the man did too. Finally the Lord stood to His feet and, reaching down His own massive hand, pulled the man onto his feet.

The man was a little unsteady at first, for he had never stood up before. Like a newly born colt, he had to figure out what to do with those lanky new legs. But he was so muscular and well-coordinated that it couldn't have taken him long. Perhaps he stood still for a moment before flexing his pectoral muscles. Then, bending over, he counted his 10 massive toes. Or, running a giant hand over his own shoulder, he jumped when he squeezed his own arm. Whatever he did, you can be sure God was helping him all the way. At some point they even started talking.

"Hello," God must have said in His rich and musical voice.

"Uh, hello!" The man opened his mouth, surprised he could make a sound. Of course, we don't know

how their conversation went. But it likely went something like this:

"My name is God. I'm your Father, and I just made you."

"Why, thank You. I'm glad to be alive!"

"You're welcome. Your name will be Adam. I want you to be My friend, and I love you very much. So I've made you a home, over here in this garden."

Taking Adam by the elbow, God took one step toward the garden. The man looked down at his two big feet. And then, watching what God did, he lifted one powerful leg and took his very first step. Then God took another step, and Adam did too. So the first human being walked with God right into the beautiful Garden of Eden.

Overwhelmed by the sights and sounds of it all, Adam hardly knew what to say. He wiggled his toes in the carpet of living green grass, then wiggled them again on the sandy shores of a lake. Picking up a furry animal, he cuddled and carried it in his arms. He drank in the simple beauty of a rose bush, smelling the fragrance of its flowers. Then, cocking his head, he listened to the warbling of a robin, a wren, and a rose-breasted grosbeak. Perhaps he even chased down a cheetah or buried his fingers in the mane of a massive lion.

Whatever he did and wherever he went, God was with him every step of the way. For this was the very first school. God was the teacher, Adam His student, and the man had a lot to learn.

"Adam, I'd like you to meet one of My new creations," God said.

"It's furry, and it likes to make that woofing sound. Does it have a name?"

"Not yet, Adam. I thought you might like to choose names, since you'll be in charge of this world. In fact, I'm setting you up as a king—the king of the Garden of Eden."

"Thank You, Father." Adam was thrilled. "I'll name this furry fellow a 'dog.'"

And so it went through the entire garden until Adam had named the elephants, giraffes, buffaloes, turtles, butterflies, dolphins, and birds. It must have been a fun job, thinking of names for all the funny, furry, and friendly creatures that lived in the Garden of Eden.

But at last it was done, and that's when Adam turned to God with a question. You see, God had created him to be a thinking, intelligent being. He could surely count, right from the start. So it didn't take long for Adam to notice that there were two of every creature in the garden—except him!

It must have been a little awkward at first—asking God about that. Adam was totally thrilled with the garden, so he didn't want to complain. But the God who made Adam had also given him the desire—the longing—to have a companion more like himself. And so Adam turned to God.

"Uh, excuse me, Father—may I ask a question?"

"Certainly!"

"Well, I just wanted to say that I'm very happy to be here, and I love all the things You have made."

"Thank you, Adam." God smiled. The human being looked questioningly into the eyes of his Creator. "But I did notice that there are, um, two hippos, two horned grebes, two herons, and two horses. I also noticed that there are two each of the gazelles, goats, and giraffes. And You know, we keep finding new and more beautiful things in the garden. So I was just wondering if, perhaps, there might be another Adam nearby. Maybe we just haven't seen it yet?"

Adam looked hopefully up at God, and the great God of the universe smiled graciously back. Then once again the Lord took Adam by the elbow.

"Come with Me, My son," He said in His deep and musical voice.

Adam didn't say much during this walk with God. He was too busy looking behind rocks and bushes, hoping to find another being like himself. Perhaps they returned to the banks of the quiet river where God had made Adam. Perhaps they stood over that human-shaped hole in the soil where Adam had breathed his first breath. And now, as Adam looked up at God and wondered what to expect, a strange sense of sleepiness swept over him. He sat down for a moment, hoping it might go away. Then he lay down, next to that hollow shaped like himself.

"I'm so tired, Father," he murmured.

"Yes," God replied. His hand was on Adam's shoulder, tucking him in for his very first nap. Adam's eyelids fluttered. Unable to fight it any longer, the very first man drifted deeper and deeper into his very first sleep.

Then the God who had made him smiled and ran His hand thoughtfully down Adam's side. In addition to being a parent, He was also a surgeon. And like so many parents who have followed, God knew that now, when His child was sleeping, was the very best time to work.

CHAPTER 14

The Very First Wedding

God could have made Eve from Adam's leftover mud—if He had wanted to. But that's not what He had in mind. The Lord wanted to do something more special and creative than *that*.

He also could have chosen an ear lobe, big toe, or finger to take from Adam's body. But He didn't, because once again, God had a wonderful plan. He wanted Adam's new "helper" to be his companion and friend. To walk and work and be by his side in the beautiful Garden of Eden. And so this special person, who was to *stand by* Adam's side, would be taken *from* his side.

The Creator made Eve from Adam's

own body, to show that she truly should be "a part" of him. He started, of course, by making Adam feel drowsy. Then God could remove, without pain, a "starter piece" from his new son's body.

It didn't take God long to find the rib He needed. After all, He had just made it. And so God unhooked a long, curving rib and closed up Adam's side. Then, while His new child was still soundly sleeping, God went to work on the rib.

Just how God turned a single rib into a beautiful woman, we surely don't know. But we do know that with God everything is possible. The Bible tells us that the same God who made the earth out of nothing, lit it up with His glory, set the stars in space and the planets in their orbits, and then decorated the earth with lilies and lilacs, now transformed Adam's rib into a woman. No doubt, just as He did with Adam, God "breathed into her nostrils the breath of life." Again there was once more the flutter of eyelashes, the first deep breath, and the look of wonder at the loving face of a Father, Creator, and Friend.

But wait! This was too good not to share. With a touch of his mighty hand God woke Adam out of his deep sleep. Adam reached for his side right away. Something was missing—he could feel it! Then it was his turn to blink and stare. My, how his rib had changed! Right away, deep in his heart, Adam knew this new person was just the one he'd been looking for. She was part of his bones and flesh, made to stand by his side. Why, this must be Mrs. Adam!

Then Adam wiggled his toes, and Eve wiggled hers. When he gave her a smile, she shot one right back. But when he leaped to his feet, she wasn't so sure about that. So, just as God had done for him, Adam reached down his hand to help. Pulling Eve up to her feet, he showed her just how to walk. And together they walked, hand in hand, into the waiting arms of God.

"Thank You, Father!" Adam must have murmured as God's hand rested once more on his shoulder.

"You're welcome, My son," the Lord replied. "And now, do you have a name for this lovely young lady?"

Adam thought for a moment.

"I think I will call her 'woman,'" he said, "for she was taken out of man" (Genesis 2:23). Later Adam would name her Eve (Genesis 3:20).

Then, wrapping the happy couple in a big bear hug, God married them right away. Of course, He also explained what marriage was all about. As the world's first couple, they were to be lovers, friends, and someday even parents. They were to care for each other, look out for each other, and work together to care for the garden—the beautiful Garden of Eden.

"The garden? What's the garden?" she must have asked.

Once again it was time for a tour, and what a tour it was. Only this time the animals had names. And this time, there was a Mrs. Adam to walk by his side.

As the sun began to set on the happy couple and their heavenly Father, God's plan for creating this world and filling it with beautiful people and places and things was perfect and complete. The Lord wouldn't have to work tomorrow—that is, He wouldn't be making new things. Instead, He would be creating a relationship with these, His two youngest children. He wanted to set aside some special family time to get better acquainted. Also He wanted to tell them many things about heaven, the world, and most of all—Himself.

And so God, in His great wisdom, declared a special holiday—or, shall we say, holy day. After a very full week and an even busier day, it was time for a change in pace. Only six days ago the world had been a watery blob of darkness. But how beautiful it was now, in the light of the setting sun.

"And God saw every thing that He had made, and, behold, it was very good. And the evening and the morning were the sixth day" (Genesis 1:31, KJV).

CHAPTER 15

A Day to Remember

You might think God was done "making" things at the end of that first Friday, and in a roundabout way, He was. He had no need to make light, air, land, trees, or flowers. Nor did God need to create turtles and tetras, parrots and pumas, indigo buntings, and even human beings. By now you would think there was nothing more to make. But in spite of all the things He had accomplished, God did have one more very important task on His to-do list on this, the seventh day of the week. God wanted to make time for Adam and Eve, His new children.

The Lord understood, right from the start, that the "family that prays together, stays together." He also knew that, though the world was fully created, His friendship with Adam, Eve, and their future children had just begun. And it takes time to build a friendship. Time to walk, talk, sing, and laugh together.

Even in the perfect Garden of Eden, where all was health and beauty, it would be possible for Adam and Eve to wander away from God. Even the best of friends who don't spend time together drift apart. And so, on the seventh day of creation, God gave His new children a very special gift: the gift of His time.

Of course, God's presence would be with His children every day of the week. And He would often visit them in the garden in the cool of the day, on Mondays, Tuesdays, and Wednesdays as well as on the seventh day. But one day of the week—the Sabbath—God would spend all day with His children.

And what a happy day it was, that very first Sabbath day. There was so much to talk about, think about, and do.

Have you ever been in a beautiful garden in which everything was so breathtaking and perfect that you hardly knew what to think? Some gardens are like that, you know. Gardens with sweet-scented bushes and lush green grasses. Or petunias and pansies, next to a winding path or a waterfall. Or park benches next to a pond, where you can watch the sun go down and come up again (if you stay there long enough).

Well, that's how gorgeous it was in the beautiful Garden of Eden. It's hard for us to even imagine how pretty it was, because we've never seen anything like it. But we can try. So close your eyes real tight, and think of the prettiest garden or place you've ever seen. Then try to imagine a place that is twice

that pretty. And after you've thought of such a wonderfully incredible place, try to imagine another that is twice as pretty as that. That's hard to do, isn't it? But if you can think of a garden that's 10 times as pretty as the grandest garden you've ever seen, then you might have at least a little idea of what God's garden was like. For it really was perfect in every way.

The Garden of Eden had no swamps, deserts, or dead trees. There weren't even any stinging scorpions, poisonous plants, or pesky bugs. No, there was only beautiful healthy life in every nook and cranny of God's grand and glorious garden.

But as beautiful as the garden was, and as much as Adam and Eve must have enjoyed it on that first wonderful Sabbath, it was nothing compared to the warmth they felt in their hearts when close to God. Something about their Maker filled them with love and happiness. He knew so much about them, the earth, and everything in it. And He was so pleasant to talk with. But most of all, Adam and Eve could see that God truly loved them. He had given them bodies and food, a mind and each other, the beautiful garden with everything in it, and the wonderful gift of His time. And so Adam and Eve responded to God's friendship by loving Him back. In fact, they adored Him—for they could see that He had their best good in mind with everything He had done.

Of course, all this happiness at the close of Creation called for a grand celebration. And so God declared that this earth-wide holiday—or holy day—should be kept at the end of each week. He would come down from heaven, and His children would put aside the ordinary things they did in the week and spend special time with Him.

Adam and Eve were probably standing in the Garden, talking about these things, when a new sound—one they had never heard before—greeted their ears. It was the heavenly angelic choir. The angels were so happy at what they had seen that they could keep silent no longer. In their hearts they knew that God was gracious and good, and now they loved Him even more for the wonderful things He had done in His creation of the earth. And so lifting their voices, they sang a song about their Friend Jesus.

Some angels strummed on their harps, while others joined in from across a cloud, playing their golden trumpets. It was all very beautiful—the most beautiful thing, save the voice of God, that Adam and Eve had heard. And heaven was very close to earth at that moment, though the best was yet to be.

"Come on down," God motioned to the leader of the heavenly choir. "There's somebody I'd like you to meet."

Beaming like the proud parent He was, God threw His arms around Adam and Eve. Together they watched as the heavenly choir filed down a cloudy set of stairs onto Planet Earth. Smiles and greetings abounded, as they joined in the very first "heavenly handshake."

As the very first Sabbath drew to a close, the angel choir leader may well have walked to where Adam and Eve stood next to God. "We'd like to sing a special song to close out the Sabbath," he said.

"Wonderful!" Adam and Eve were thrilled. The

choir leader was silent for a moment. He looked first at Adam, then Eve, as if sizing them up.

"Will you join us?" he finally said.

The first man and woman looked questioningly at God. They hadn't thought of singing before. Could it be that in addition to the joys of walking, talking, eating, working, and playing—that they could also sing?

"Hmmmmm . . ." Adam was deep in thought, but Eve was already humming a little tune. God nodded and smiled.

"Yes, you can." He said simply.

"You won't need any music," the angel explained. "We're doing an antiphonal number. That means we will sing across the clouds to you, and whatever we sing, you sing back."

"We'll try," Adam and Eve agreed. The angel motioned to the heavenly choir. Without a word, they began filing onto the billowing cloud that would take them back to heaven. Then, at just the right instant, they turned back and broke into glorious song.

"Holy, Holy, Holy, Lord God Almighty," they sang. "Early in the morning our songs shall rise to Thee." There was an expectant pause, as Adam looked at Eve. Then, falling on his knees before God, Adam started in with a strong voice.

"Holy, Holy, Holy, Lord God Almighty." A beautiful voice sang with him, and Adam knew it was Eve. "Early in the morning our songs shall rise to Thee." Back and forth they sang, as the angelic choir rose up to the gates of heaven.

"Only Thou art holy, merciful and mighty. Perfect in power, in love and purity."

Tears of joy streamed down Adam's face when

the song was over. He was so happy. Then He felt a hand on his shoulder. It was God, telling His children goodnight. There would be other days, other songs to sing. And they would have many more Sabbaths to spend together, for God had set aside the seventh day of each week just for that special purpose.

"Thus the heavens and the earth were finished, and all the host of them. And on the seventh day God ended his work which he had made; and he rested on the seventh day from all his work which he had made. And God blessed the seventh day, and sanctified it: because that in it he had rested from all his work which God created and made" (Genesis 2:1-3, KJV).

CHAPTER 16

The Way Things Ought to Be

From what we have read so far about life in the Garden of Eden, you may have noticed that God set things up in a certain way. Knowing what was best for His creatures, He planned everything out so that even the tiniest ant could have a happy and peaceful life. Of course, life was much different on Planet Earth during those glad, happy days in the Garden of Eden. For one thing, there was no death. Because the garden had no death, it also had no sadness.

Nor did God's children spend much time talking about rules back then, either, for everything was set-up to run in its natural order. God had written His holy law in the hearts of Adam and Eve, so it came naturally to them to be kind and loving and gentle. Anyway, they were too much in love to say mean things to each other. Probably they did call each other names from time to time, but no doubt they were sweet ones like "honey" or "sugar" or "precious."

The animals were all kind to each other as well. The lions thought lambs were so cute that they wouldn't think of putting one on their dinner plate. The birds ate berries instead of beetles, the grizzlies ate grass instead of fish, and so it went through the whole happy creation. And though they didn't know it, they were all reflecting the kindness and love that God had shown to them.

Of course, Lucifer the fallen angel wouldn't want you to know all this. "God is mean," he had told the heavenly angels. He would like you to think that God set up a huge book with five million rules right in the middle of the garden. That He took Adam and Eve to it and, after reading every single rule, banged His fist on the book, thundering "Keep them or else!"

But as we know, nothing could be farther from the truth. God did give Adam and Eve one rule right from the beginning. He asked them not to eat from one special tree in the garden. But that was not any big sacrifice, because they had hundreds and maybe even thousands of other trees they could eat from. But this tree, called the "Tree of Knowledge of Good and Evil," He had put in the garden as a simple test.

God needed to know if Adam and Eve would trust Him enough to obey Him. If they would prove loyal on this little point, then He would know that they were willing to obey Him on many other things. He was raising children who would love and honor God and, someday, would fill the courts of heaven with happy songs.

But if the first couple should fail on this one simple test, it would show that they didn't trust God. More than that, to fail was to fall from the high place God had already given them, so that in their own strength they couldn't be trusted to carry out the great plans He had for their lives.

Other than this one simple rule, the Garden of Eden didn't have many regulations. God didn't "command" Adam and Eve to keep the Sabbath. He didn't have to—they loved to spend time with Him. God didn't set a certain bedtime for Adam and Eve. Instead, He just let the sun sink into the west at a certain time each day. And, being the very intelligent humans they were, Adam and Eve knew what to do.

Nor did God have to tell Adam not to marry more than one wife. When it comes to marriage, He knew that three is truly a crowd. For the happiness of all involved, there should only be two peas in the marriage pod.

We can also learn much from the kind of food the couple ate. If creation had been left to some children, no doubt all the pine trees would have been popsicles. Lily pads could have been pizzas, waterfalls could have thundered red soda pop, and even the dirt itself would be rich chocolate cake. But God filled His new world with healthy things.

It would have been interesting to be in the Garden of Eden the first time Adam's stomach rumbled. It must have been a big rumble, for he surely had a large stomach.

"Um, excuse me, Father," he might have said. "I

have this strange feeling, right in the pit of my stomach."

Of course, God gave him a knowing look and ordered some root beer, cheese munchies, and a wet burrito right away.

"Wait a minute!" you say. "My Bible says Adam ate fruit, nuts, and grains." And you're right. So God and Adam probably took a stroll through the garden, picking a bucket of blueberries or almonds or walnuts. Then, perhaps using a huge slab of gold for their table, they shared the very first meal on Planet Earth. If Eve was with them by this time, she might have helped decorate the table.

We really don't know the details, but we do know some things for sure. They couldn't possibly have had a pig roast, fish fry, or a picnic of fried chicken, because there was no death in the garden. Probably they didn't have stir fry, french fries, or any other type of fries either. While they might have had a banana split, it was not the kind you're thinking of.

Nor did they pig out, for one could hardly imagine them lolling around the garden with stomachs so full they could hardly move. No, they ate the right amounts of the right things, just as God had planned for them to. And the fruits were delicious, the nuts were nutritious, and surely it all tasted 10 times better than the very best birthday dinner you could imagine.

Adam and Eve didn't entertain themselves in the same way we do today, either. They loved to work with their hands in the garden, and God gave them very special jobs to do, such as training the vines into beautiful bowers and planting petunias in all the best places. Perhaps they even made tunnels through bushes, or decorated a "secret" room just under a waterfall. Whatever work they did, it was pleasant, and they enjoyed it.

It's hard to imagine them sunk into a bed of moss, glued to a movie of someone's make-believe life. They were too busy living their own! Their life, though simple, was the happiest life that humanity has ever known.

God could have set up video arcades, amusement parks, and the grandest theater ever. But He didn't. Adam and Eve could have e-mailed the angels, surfed the "Universal Web," and networked electronically under a well-wired tree. But they didn't.

God did wear a pager, however. Even when He was in heaven, His ears were always open to the thoughts, feelings, and prayers of Adam and Eve. Yes, there is much we can learn from life in the Garden of Eden. For there, in that beautiful garden, God showed (rather than preached) one of the greatest sermons our world has ever heard. By setting an example in His own quiet way, God was showing us all the way things ought to be.

CHAPTER 17

Satan Feels "Sorry"

Sad to say, all the happiness in the Garden of Eden made Satan very jealous. When he heard Adam and Eve singing their happy duets, he thought of his own wonderful voice. As Adam smiled gently at Eve, Satan remembered how happy he'd once been himself. And when he saw the contented couple snuggling in some cozy little nook, it made his stomach churn.

Satan's plans for his own life had really flopped. It's hard to imagine how grumpy he must have felt, but he was very upset about how things had turned out.

He had gambled a lot to rebel against God—risked it all and lost. Not only did he lose his job as head angel, he had thought all God's angels would join him. Only a third took his side, however. The

74

devil believed that he'd be happy if he was in charge, but instead he was very depressed. Most of all, Satan had gambled that he could stay in heaven and still get his way. That he, not God, would rule under the emerald rainbow. That all the angels would bow and sing praises to him, cheerfully doing his word.

But though Satan did rule the rebellious angels, his dreams lay in heaps all about him. He was an outcast, forever expelled from the pearly gates. His face, which had once been so peaceful, was now brooding, sullen, and angry.

Satan's angels were angry and hateful, too. They were angry at him for talking them into rebellion, angry at themselves for being so foolish, and angry at God for throwing them out.

"You'll be happy with me," Satan had promised, deceiving them with his smooth words. To their great disappointment they quickly found out that he was wrong. And they were especially horrified at the heart-wrenching thought that they had lost all heaven forever.

It's hard to imagine just how bad Satan did feel. But as he watched Adam and Eve in the Garden of Eden, he realized how much he had thrown away. And he was incredibly jealous of God's two very special friends. He wanted to be the commander *inside* of heaven—not *outside*. Satan wanted to rise to a higher position, not lower. But now he found himself a stranger and outcast, far from the warmth of the heavenly courts where he had once loved to sing.

One day, as Satan was slouching bleakly in outer space, one of God's angels whooshed by.

"Hey, come back here," Satan called after him. "I need to say something to Jesus."

The angel turned, a look of surprise on his face. And Satan recognized that face. Why, he'd sung a duet with the angel once, back in the heavenly choir. For a moment, Satan turned off his sneering voice and spoke ever so politely to the angel.

"Could you take a message to heaven for me?" the rebel leader asked. "I have something to say to Jesus."

Smiling graciously, the angel nodded. And then he was gone.

Moments later, he returned with a message from heaven. Jesus would speak with Satan! The devil had his speech all ready for the occasion, for he had had many hours to think about it.

"I want to come back to heaven," Satan said. "If you'll just let me have my old job back again, I won't be a rebel anymore."

Tears streamed down Jesus' face as He heard Satan's words, for he knew Satan couldn't return. God had been very patient with His wayward angel. Even after Satan started spreading his wrong ideas to the other angels, God had given him lots of time, hoping the wandering angel would become loyal again. The Lord had also asked him to change his ways many times, but the highest angel had always refused.

Then came the day when Lucifer received his last opportunity—his very last chance. Once again he said no. More than that, he continued to deceive the other angels—angels who would never had dreamed an evil thought had it not been for him. Jesus looked into Satan's heart and knew there was still a rebel inside. He also realized that Satan was only sorry for what he had lost—not what he had done. And so the answer was no. Lucifer had become Satan. And sad as it was, he had gone too far to return to heaven.

CHAPTER 18

The Diabolical Plan

The bad angels watched as Satan hurled meteors through the wastelands of space. By the way he was acting, they knew what had happened. As with Satan, God had also given them many chances to resume their loyalty to God, but they had said no. They had watered the seed of rebellion until it had crowded out the good seeds in their hearts. Like Satan, they had gone too far to return.

After wearing himself out on a punching-bag planet, Satan stomped off into deeper space. He needed some time by himself—some brooding time to plan his next move in the horrible game he had started.

It was then, when Satan was sulking about what to do next, that he hatched a horrendous idea. He would trick God's happy new couple! The devil would plunge them into rebelling just as he had done! Their blissfulness destroyed, they would then share his sorry state.

The idea was so wicked that it even scared Satan at first. But though he at first shuddered at the thought of such a diabolical deed, he quickly shoved such thoughts from his mind.

"If heaven's not happy *with me*," he sneered, "I'll make sure it's sad *without me*." In the back of his mind Satan hoped God could still forgive him. That He would make a way for Adam and Eve to escape the results of their sin and include the devil in it. But if God didn't, Satan was prepared to fight. If he couldn't be king of heaven, he would set up his own kingdom on God's new planet. Then, if he and his fellow rebels could only eat the fruit of the tree of life, they could live forever. And then Satan, not Adam, would be ruler of the Garden of Eden.

When Satan first shared his plan with his followers, they shrank from the very idea. But as usual, he was a great persuader.

"It's our only hope," he urged the fallen angels. "Without it, we're doomed."

Then the fallen angels went off by themselves for a while. They, too, needed time to think and talk things over. When they came back, their faces reflected the anger and hate of their leader.

"We'll help you," they snarled. "That way we'll all get even with God."

And that's how the fallen angels became evil angels, Satan's workers to cause sadness and suffering in our world.

Of course, we can only imagine how God felt at that moment. He must have looked down from

heaven and sighed, for He knew what Satan did not—
that the battle in heaven was over, but the war for
our planet was only beginning.

CHAPTER 19

Alarm Bells
in Heaven

Ta-eeeee! Ta-eeeee! God's sentries blew warning blasts on their golden trumpets as they swept through the gates of heaven. Instantly the entire city leaped into action. Angels zipped to their posts, gates snapped shut, and the entire city pulsed into its high alert state.

"What's going on?" whispered one angel, perched in his portal, to another.

"It's Satan again," came the reply. "He wants to attack the Garden of Eden."

"You mean blow it to bits?"

"Worse than that. He wants to trick Adam and Eve—to get them to sin. He wants to make them sad, God sad, and all heaven sad all over again. And he wants to be king of the Garden of Eden instead of Adam."

"Oh no!" The angels who heard it burst into tears.

"Oh yes!" the angel who told it replied. High above them, under the emerald rainbow, God's sentries were already spreading the word. Of course, they didn't have to tell God what Satan was doing. The Lord already knew. In fact, He was in a meeting with Jesus at that very moment, deciding how to handle Satan's attack.

Whoosh! Two of God's fastest angels zoomed out the pearly portals. They were on an important mission—a mission to warn Planet Earth. In the meantime, Satan was perfecting his terrible plan.

"I know I'll get my chance," he laughed to his followers. "God wants love, not slaves, so He'll let *them* decide."

"But what if they tell you no?" Satan's head henchman worried.

"Then they'll be stronger to resist me," Satan wrinkled his wicked forehead, his face filled with hate.

"But I'll trick them," he shouted. "That's what I'll do." He sneered at the evil angels.

"You guys aren't smart enough for this job," he snarled. "I'll have to do it myself!" And with that he stormed off to plot his wicked deed. To prepare his attack on Adam and Eve he began spying on them.

Sometimes, when they were alone in the garden, Satan would sneak in himself. Since the tree of knowledge of good and evil was the only place he could go in the garden, that's where he always went. From his perch in the tree, he would listen to the happy couple singing praises to God. Satan also saw Adam and

Eve talking with God and noticed how much they loved Him.

Then, with a heart full of hatred, he would storm off to work on his wicked plot. More than anything else, Satan wanted to change their songs into sobbing and their happiness into tears. And so he perfected his wicked and evil plan. Guessing that God would warn Adam and Eve about his designs, Satan decided to try a sneak (or should we say, "snake") attack.

Of course, God's speedy angels had already sounded alarms in Eden.

"Be careful," the angels warned Adam and Eve. "Satan, God's enemy, wants to get you to be on his side." They told the couple about the beauty of Lucifer, his pride, and his terrible fall. The good angels also taught Adam and Eve more about God's law and how it's as special as God Himself.

"His rules are good and fair," the angels said. "They show how the entire universe should run."

"When somebody breaks God's law," the angels explained, "death is the sure result. So please, for the good of yourselves and the entire world, please don't break God's law."

Although God wanted Adam and Eve to understand how important His law was, the decision of whether or not to obey had to be up to them. They could choose to obey God's law and live, or disobey and die. For just as surely as somebody who jumps up comes back down, somebody who sins will perish.

It was very sad, of course, for Adam and Eve even to think about such things. But they had to understand how important it was to keep God's law.

"Satan wants you to disobey God's law," the

angels told Adam and Eve. "He even wants to hurt you. But as long as you obey God, he won't be allowed to harm you."

If needed, every angel in heaven would fly to the couple's rescue. And if they said no to Satan the first time, they would be stronger than ever. Someday, if they proved true to God, he wouldn't even be allowed to tempt them anymore.

But sadly, if they said yes to Satan even once, they would be changed. Because they had sinned, they would never be the same again. Then they wouldn't have power to tell Satan no by themselves.

God didn't let Satan follow Adam and Eve all over the Garden of Eden and constantly bother them. He wanted to make it as easy as possible for his youngest children to obey. But they did have to make a choice one way or another.

So God had set up the tree of knowledge of good and evil in the Garden of Eden as a simple "test" for Adam and Eve. If they went near the tree and Satan tempted them there, the choice they made would show whom they trusted the most—Satan or God.

Adam and Eve understood very well that they weren't to eat . To do so would be to disobey God. And if they disobeyed, they knew they would die.

CHAPTER 20

The Wily Intruder

Be careful," the angels told Adam and Eve as they left the garden. "Remember, Eve, to stay close to Adam." As long as Adam and Eve remained together, they would be stronger to resist Satan's tricks.

But one beautiful springlike day, while Eve was working in the garden, she somehow wandered away from Adam's side. She didn't notice what she had done at first, but soon she realized that she was alone. For the first time in her life, fear gripped her heart. She should have run back to Adam right then, but she didn't. Instead, she pushed those fearful thoughts out of her mind.

"I think I'm wise enough to know if Satan should come around," Eve said to herself. "If he does show up, I'll just tell him no."

It was then,

of course, that Satan had his big chance. He didn't make it easy for Eve, either. It wasn't his style to walk up and say, "Hello, I'm Satan." Oh no. He didn't even dress like an angel. Instead, he found one of the prettiest animals in the garden—a colorful, flying creature that Adam had named a "serpent." Satan dressed himself up like the serpent. Then he went and sat in the forbidden tree—the tree of the knowledge of good and evil.

It wasn't long before Eve, who was now quite a ways from Adam, wandered by. Forgetting what the angel said, she soon found herself staring at the beautiful tree with its scrumptious-looking fruit.

"I wonder why God doesn't want us to eat this fruit," Eve said out loud.

Satan smiled from inside the serpent disguise, and it was a wicked, hateful smile. Here was the chance he'd been waiting for, and he knew it.

"Hello!" Satan spoke through the snake in his most musical voice. "Did God say you shouldn't eat of every tree in this garden?"

"Oh!" The voice scared Eve so that she nearly jumped out of her skin. She had thought she was alone, and she certainly wasn't expecting to hear a serpent speak! Eve was even more surprised to hear the serpent say exactly what she'd been thinking. The serpent continued to talk in its soothing, friendly voice.

"My, how beautiful you are," it murmured, and Eve blushed. She had no idea the serpent was Satan, but she sure liked the things it said.

"We can eat fruit from every tree in the garden," Eve explained to the creature. "But we can't eat from this tree. God told us not to. If we do, we'll die."

The serpent dropped his jaw in amazement.

"You won't really die," he lied. "God knows that if you eat this fruit, you'll become a god like Him. That's why He doesn't want you to eat it. Why, if you take a bite of this fruit, you'll know the difference between good and bad."

Then Satan the serpent reached out and picked the most luscious piece of fruit he could find. Taking a big bite out of the juiciest part, he smiled down at her.

"If you eat some of this fruit," he said, "you'll be wiser and smarter than you've ever been before. Why, this fruit is the very reason why I, a serpent, can talk at all."

The serpent stretched his colorful feathers, edging his face toward Eve's as if to tell some wonderful secret.

"As you can see, I'm not dead!" he whispered. Satan held a piece of the fatal fruit closer, closer, and still closer to Eve's slender fingers.

"God wouldn't let you *die* if you eat the fruit," the father of lies went on. "He was just trying to scare you. How could you possibly die, anyway? Haven't you already eaten from the tree of life?"

Eve had made a huge mistake in wandering from Adam's side. Now she did another one in talking to Satan. And she made a third big mistake in listening to his arguments. The serpent seemed so convincing that Eve began to believe what he said. And this meant that she didn't believe God. She believed a lie instead of the truth.

Sad to say, Satan is trying to do the same thing to us today. He wants us to think we'll be happier and better off if we break God's holy law. Satan didn't tell

Eve all the sad things that had happened to him because of what he'd done, and he won't tell you that today, either.

It was then, after his latest lie, that Satan as the serpent handed some fruit to Eve. And without even thinking, she reached out and took it.

"There, you *touched* it!" the serpent cocked his head, looking wise. "Are you *dead?*" he wanted to know.

Seeing that nothing bad had happened to her, Eve became bolder.

If I touched the fruit and didn't die, she thought, *I might as well just eat it.*

She took a bite, and it was very delicious. Then Eve took another bite, and another. And as she did, somehow she felt she was smarter and wiser than she had been before. It was as if something wonderful was happening inside her body—or so she thought.

Grabbing a handful of the forbidden fruit, Eve dashed down a path through the garden. Now that it was too late, she was looking for Adam, her husband.

CHAPTER 21

How Eve Helped the Devil

A dam, Adam!" Eve cried.
Adam didn't know what to think when she ran up. She was excited, yet in a very strange sort of way. He'd never seen her act like this, and he was even more amazed to find that Eve had eaten the forbidden fruit.

"The serpent! The serpent!" Adam shook his head in disbelief as Eve told her story. "That must be Satan— the one God warned us about."

"You won't die if you eat this fruit," she tried to reassure him. "See, I'm just fine!" She twirled around. He looked on thought- fully, his hand on his chin.

"You're as beautiful as ever, my dear,"

he sighed. "But why, oh why didn't we stay together? I should have come looking for you, the very first moment I missed you."

Eve ran her fingers down his muscle-bound arm.

"Don't worry about me!" she purred. "I don't think God's unhappy with me. In fact, I feel wonderful—better than ever before!"

The serpent had tricked Eve. She did not know who the serpent was or what he was up to. But Adam knew exactly what was going on that terrible day. He knew that she had broken God's law. That God had given them just a little test, and that she had failed it. Then a terrible argument raged in Adam's mind.

What will ever become of you? Tears streamed down his handsome face as he bent and kissed Eve on the nose.

What will happen to our marriage if you sin and I don't? Adam's thoughts raced to the now-uncertain future. *Will we still be together?* He loved God, and he loved the angels. But somehow, in that terrible moment of temptation, he loved Eve even more. She was part of him—he couldn't imagine being without her.

Quickly Adam made up his mind. He would die with Eve! Grabbing a piece of fruit from her hands, he bit into it. Just then, for one fleeting moment, a strange thrill coursed through his body.

Maybe, just maybe, something wonderful has happened, Adam tried to convince himself. But then, as the terrible truth dawned in his aching heart, the thrill turned into a chill. Adam started to think about his sin. He had disobeyed God and was afraid, so afraid. Then he looked at Eve—the one he had loved so much, the one he thought he could die for. Now,

for the very first time in their marriage, he felt angry at her.

And their robes! Their beautiful, warmth-filled robes of light were fading off their bodies! The air around them grew chillier by the second, making the forlorn couple feel undressed inside and out. That's when Adam and Eve started to realize how bad sin really was.

"You shouldn't have left my side," he scolded.

"You could have reminded me," Eve snapped, and Adam sighed. They were fighting already!

"God is so good and kind," Adam reasoned, "maybe He'll forgive just this one sin. Then we won't have to die."

Eve reached for some fig leaves.

"Stop thinking and get to work," she ordered. Together they broke off giant green leaves, sewing them together by the stems. Of course, even their nimble fingers couldn't make anything like the garments of light they had just lost. Their new clothes covered them about as well as the feeble excuses they were now trying to make.

"Do you think God will notice that we changed our clothes?" Eve wanted to know.

"How could He *help* but notice," Adam shot back. Fiddling with fig leafs wasn't his idea of a good time, especially these slippery, stubborn stems.

"Oh, how in the world will I ever tell God what we've done?"

CHAPTER 22

The Costly Decision

Of course, Adam didn't need to tell God the terrible news of what had happened in the Garden of Eden. The Lord already knew, and so did the angels. They had watched from the gates of heaven as the whole sorry scene unfolded.

The heavenly choir had just been warming up for another concert, but their song had stopped when they heard that Satan was making his move. Breathlessly they peeked past the portals of the holy city, hoping that Adam and Eve would make the right choice. They watched Eve wander from Adam's side and heard her talking to Satan in his disguise as the serpent. Tears streamed down their faces when Eve first touched the forbidden fruit, then carried some off to Adam.

"I can't believe they'd do that," one angel exclaimed as Adam bit off a juicy chunk.

"After everything God's done for them," others said as they turned away in disgust. A black cloud of grief hung over the heavenly courts as sadness, shock, and disbelief filled millions of angel faces. Then there was sobbing in heaven, worse than what happens at even the saddest funeral. The angels, who had already been through one war in heaven, knew what Adam's sin meant. Death to the sinner, death to the one who broke God's law, death to Adam and Eve.

"We must tell God about this." The mightiest angel in heaven grabbed the arm of another.

"Yes," his friend agreed. And off they flew to the throne room under the emerald rainbow.

Of course, God already knew what had happened. And though He loved Adam and Eve very much, He also had to uphold His holy law. But before God could execute the sentence of death, Jesus, God's only Son, said, "Let me take their place, Father. They made a dreadful mistake, but they're not like Satan, the one who knew You so well and still managed to start it all. If You'll let me take their penalty—pay their price—I think I can win them back."

A deep conversation took place in the heavenly throne room that day. God loved Adam and Eve very much, but He didn't want to give up His Son. It was a huge sacrifice for Jesus, too, for the very thought of death filled His heart with horror. But His love for Adam and Eve was so strong that He wanted to save them anyway He could.

At last the Father and the Son made Their decision. They had a plan in place. Jesus would die so

Adam and Eve could live. Walking out of the throne room, Jesus called a huge assembly of all the heavenly angels.

"I'm going to die for Adam and Eve," He announced. Then He described what He was willing to do to save humans and how very low He would have to stoop.

The news shocked the angels.

"No, no, no!" cried the angel chorus. They loved Jesus with all their hearts. The thought of Him dying or even suffering was more than they could take.

"Please don't die for their sins." The mightiest angel in heaven fell at the feet of Jesus. "Let me go instead."

"No, let me!" another exclaimed. "Let me, let me, let me!" Gods' good angels were so loving and unselfish that they were willing to give up their own lives so Adam and Eve could live.

Of course, an angel could never have paid the price. For only one who's as special as God's law itself—only God—could pay the penalty for humanity. But though an angel could never die to save humanity, God did have a job for His heavenly helpers. When Jesus became a human, the angels would be stronger than Him. So they could help Him and even comfort Him when He was hurting. They could also go back and forth between heaven and earth, carrying messages between God and His children. And they could guard God's children from the power of Satan's angels, helping them choose what was right.

"It will turn out all right," Jesus told the angels. "When I go to earth and die, I'll save many people. And because of my victory, someday there'll be no more sin. In the meantime, everyone will see how terrible sin really is. So once sin is banished, it will never come back again."

Then joy once more filled heaven. Though the angels knew the terrible things that would happen someday, they also understood that God would win in the end. Humanity would be saved and would come once more to the beautiful Garden of Eden.

Pulling out their harps, the angelic choir sang a new song. Who knows, maybe it was the same tune they would someday sing on the hills of Bethlehem.

"Glory to God in the highest, and on earth peace, good will toward men." Yes, when they realized how much God really loved man, and what He was willing to do to save him, "the morning stars sang together, and all the sons of God shouted for joy" (Job 38:7, KJV).

The celebration was still going on in heaven when God pulled his fiery chariot out of the palace garage. He'd always told the angels how much He loved them. Now it was time to show that love in a deeper way than He'd ever done before.

Leaving behind the emerald rainbow, God headed for the little blue planet called Earth. It was time for His daily visit, time for a talk in the garden, time to put His own wonderful kind of love into action. No doubt He felt horrible as He left the gates of Heaven, for it was also time for the tough dose of discipline only this Father could give.

CHAPTER 23

Footsteps
in the Garden

It must be quite an impressive sight when God travels. If you don't think so, just read the book of Ezekiel. There the prophet describes a chariot of fire surrounded by smoke and voices crying "Holy, Holy, Holy." With a set of small wheels moving inside bigger wheels, and creatures and lightning and a whirlwind, it was an awesome sight to behold. This was the chariot God rode in during Ezekiel's vision, and we don't know for sure, but He may very well have also traveled in it to see Adam and Eve.

But though our God is an awesome God, He didn't want to scare Adam and Eve. Knowing how nervous they must have felt at the moment, He probably parked his chariot somewhere outside the garden gate and walked in on foot.

Adam and Eve were just sewing the last of their fig leaves into place when they heard a familiar voice calling them by name.

"Adam! Eve! Where are you?"

"It's God!" Adam whispered as he dived for the nearby bushes. "He's come to the garden to see us."

Now, God loved Adam and Eve, so He came to see them quite often. And they were always thrilled to see Him. In fact, they usually ran to His side.

"Adam! Where are you?" He called again in His deep, musical voice.

Adam was just ducking deeper under a lilac bush when He felt someone standing over him! God parted the branches.

"Adam, why didn't you answer Me?" Sadness filled God's voice, though His face was still gentle and kind.

"I—I—I heard Your voice," Adam stuttered and stammered. "But I was afraid, because I wasn't dressed to meet You. So I hid myself."

"Who told you that you were undressed?" God asked. "Did you eat from *that* tree?" The Lord nodded toward the tree of knowledge of good and evil. "You know, the tree I told you not to eat from."

Adam had no excuses, and he knew it. It was also obvious that he couldn't hide from God, so he switched to a new tact—the "Blame Game."

Eve was just emerging from her hiding place when Adam caught sight of her.

"The woman You gave me," he pointed. *"She* gave me the fruit, and I ate it."

In other words, it was Eve's fault. Even more than that, Adam was even blaming God for giving him Eve in the first place!

Sadly, God turned to her.

"What did *you* do?" He asked quietly. Of course, He already knew the answer to that question. But like the wise Father He was and still is, He wanted to hear the truth from the lips of His child.

Together they walked along the paths of the garden, across a meadow, past a rippling stream, and perhaps by the spot where God had given them both the gift of life. Soon they stood by the tree of knowledge of good and evil, where Satan in the disguise of the serpent still sat, sunning happily on a huge branch.

"The serpent," Eve pointed at Satan. "He tricked me, and so I ate." Like Adam, she wanted to play the blame game. She was trying to say that her sin was the serpent's fault, and, in a roundabout way, that of God who had made the serpent.

"Why did God let the serpent into the garden, anyway?" was the unspoken question she asked.

The Lord sighed. How He loved these two foolish children of His. And how He wished He could back up the hands of time and undo their unwise decision. But He couldn't do so and still allow them the power to choose. And now there was nothing left to do. They would have to be punished for their disobedience. But first, He had a word for the serpent.

"Because you did this," He said, "you'll be cursed. You won't be pretty or fly anymore. You'll crawl on your belly, eating dust all the days of your life." And that's how the serpent—once one of God's most gorgeous creations—became a snake.

Then God looked inside the serpent, for He knew who was hiding there.

"You and the woman won't like each other," He said to Satan. "Your children and hers won't be friends.

"A child of the woman will bruise your head," God went on. Adam and Eve didn't understand it then, but He was talking about Jesus. Someday Jesus would come as a "Son of Man"—a great-great-and very-great grandchild of Adam and Eve. Right there in the garden, God told the human race that Jesus would someday come to this world and win the war with Satan, or "bruise his head."

Next God had a punishment for Eve as well. In the beginning, He had taken her from Adam's side to be the man's equal. But now, in a world of sin, one of them would have to be the leader. And God chose Adam to head up their home.

When God told Eve it would hurt to have her babies, she cried at the very thought. And up in heaven, the angels were crying, too. But God wasn't done yet, for He had a punishment for Adam as well.

"Because you listened to Eve," He said, "the ground will be cursed. There'll be crabgrass growing with your gardenias, thorns will pop up in your roses. Your peach trees won't grow as many peaches as they did before. The oranges will be smaller and not as good.

"Your work won't be fun like it used to be. In fact, you'll have to sweat to earn your living until the day you die and your body returns to the ground. For that's what I made you out of: dust you are, and because you have sinned, to the dust you will return."

Adam had been king over all the animals of the

earth. But now, because of his choice to disobey God, the animals would also rebel against him. The whole earth would show the marks of Adam and Eve's terrible, terrible sin.

When Adam and Eve heard their punishment, they could hardly believe their ears. It seemed like a terrible nightmare. Yet when they looked at the tears streaming down the face of God, they knew it was true. Falling at His feet, they begged His forgiveness.

The Lord put His hands on their shoulders. He had much to tell them about love and forgiveness, but not yet. For there was even more punishment to come, worse than anything God had mentioned so far.

CHAPTER 24

Goodbye,
Gorgeous Garden

Sometimes a change in pace also means a change in place. That's what happened to Lucifer the fallen angel. After he sinned and rebelled against God, Lucifer had to move out of heaven. And after they sinned, Adam and Eve had to leave the beautiful Garden of Eden.

Of course, they didn't want to go.

"Please let us stay," they begged God. "If You'll only let us stay, we'll obey You forever."

Then God explained to Adam and Eve that their one sin had changed them. Even if they wanted to obey, they couldn't do it in their own power. By believing Satan instead of God, they had chosen Satan. And now

Satan, not Adam, was the "prince of this world"—the king of the Garden of Eden.

Eve's heart was broken, and so was Adam's. The day was nearly over as they smelled the lilac bushes, heard the owls hooting, and walked down the winding, flower-filled paths of the Garden of Eden for the very last time. And the sun was setting, not only on the Garden of Eden, but on the happiest days our world would know for years and years to come.

God also shared in their sadness, for He never wanted Adam and Eve to sin or suffer or die. It was not in His plan for them to do wrong. He had wanted them to know only good, not evil. But they had chosen to disobey, and God had to let them suffer the terrible penalty of their sin.

Some people think about all the horrible things that have happened on our earth since that one "little" sin, and they don't understand.

"All Adam and Eve did was eat one piece of fruit," they say. And they don't think it's fair. But if they thought about it a little more deeply, they might understand. God made Adam and Eve perfect, like the angels, and gave them a very easy test. The fact that they failed such a simple test made their sin all the bigger. We also have to ask ourselves the question: "If Adam didn't pass such a little test, how could he pass a bigger one?"

Here's another thing to think about: If God had given Adam a very hard test and he had failed, some people today might have thought that God didn't care so much about the "little things." But God wants us to know that all sins are wrong, even "little" ones.

In the end, the punishments God gave Adam and

Eve were actually a blessing. The hard work they would have to do to raise food to feed their children would keep them busy and turn their hearts to God. Even the sad times—the times of tears and sorrow—would draw them closer to Him.

Although Adam and Eve didn't die that very day, they started down the road toward death. Satan had hoped that Adam and Eve would eat from the tree of life after their sin. Then somehow, he hoped, they and their sin would live forever. But God didn't want sin to last forever. So right away He sent mighty angels to guard the tree of life.

As Adam and Eve left the garden they couldn't help noticing the changes already around them. The air seemed chilly, and they shivered. The seasons started to change every few months, and as fall came, the leaves began to droop and fall from the trees. Some of the animals even started to kill each other for food.

"Oh, look, Eve," Adam must have said when he found the first fallen leaf. "It's dying!" Tears streamed down his face as he handed the giant leaf, which had once been a golden green, to Eve. Now it was an ugly, shriveled-up brown.

She burst into tears, and the two cried together. In fact, they sobbed over that one sorry little leaf.

"Is this what death is?" Eve wanted to know. "It's so horrible!"

Of course, that was only the beginning. Every day they found some new reminder of sin and the death it would bring to the earth.

But though Adam and Eve had to move out of the Garden of Eden, God in His great mercy didn't take the garden away from the earth right then. They could still come and look through its gates, catching a glimpse of the things they had lost. There, at the gate of the garden, Adam and his sons came to worship God. As they promised to obey God, there God showed them by His presence that He still loved and cared for them.

It wasn't until many years later—just before the great flood—that God removed the Garden of Eden for good. But someday He will bring it back again. And if we love Jesus enough to keep His commandments, we will walk the paths of that garden.

Breathing it's clear, pure air, we'll sit under the tree of life. And there, in this beautiful garden, we'll understand how gorgeous the earth really was when God first made it, and what it would have been like forever if Adam and Eve hadn't eaten that "one piece of fruit."

CHAPTER 25

"This Little Lamb Must *Die!*"

Whoosh! God's angel teachers stayed pretty busy after the fall of Adam and Eve. They had a lot to share with them about how God was going to save them.

When God had first made Adam and Eve they had walked and talked with Him as His personal friends. But sin drove a wedge between Him and His children. Because God was so holy, and His children so sinful, they couldn't be together in the same way as before. But He still sent the angels to talk with Adam and Eve.

"God loves you," was the message each one of them brought. "In spite of your great sin, He won't give you up to Satan. God has a plan for your life."

If Adam and his family would love Jesus, trusting Him to help them live lives that were good and kind and true, they would remain as children of God. But they must be sorry for their sins, loving God enough to obey Him, to be saved.

When the first couple realized that Jesus must die for their sins, they felt worse than ever.

"Let us die instead," they begged. "Let us die instead of Jesus."

"We've already offered," the angels sighed. "But only one who is as holy as God's law itself—like Jesus—can pay the price.

"God's law is so holy, and it never changes," the angels explained. "That's why there's such a high price for breaking it. However, Jesus loves you so much that He wants to die for you. He wants to save you, so you can come back to Him."

The angels told Adam about many important things that would someday happen. You might even say that he was a prophet, for the angels described the Flood, the second coming of Christ, and many other future events many years before they happened. Also the angels explained that while Jesus' sacrifice would be enough to save everybody, many people would choose to sin rather than live obediently.

"Because of sin, there'll be lots of pain and sorrow in this world," they said. "People will get sick more often. They won't grow as tall, and they won't be as strong as you are." In fact, human beings would sink so low that they wouldn't even be able to understand all the wonderful things God wanted to tell them. Yet Jesus, when He did come, would be so strong that He could help everyone who really believed in Him. And there would always be some people who would be true to Jesus, no matter what Satan did.

Then the angels walked to where Adam and Eve kept their animals.

"Can you show us your finest lamb?" they asked. "The very best one you have?"

"Yes," Adam answered proudly. Picking up a woolly little fellow in his arms, he held him out to the angels.

"He is so beautiful," murmured one of the angels, stroking the woolly lamb's head. Then, tears streaming down his face, he turned back to Adam.

"What's the matter?" Adam wanted to know.

"The lamb must die," the angel said simply. "It's the only way."

Eve covered her mouth, squelching the scream she wanted so badly to make.

"Wh—why—why?" Adam couldn't believe it. "What has it done?"

"That's the point," the angel answered. "It hasn't done anything. Like Jesus, the lamb is completely innocent of your sin. But Jesus must die, because you sinned. It's important for you to understand just how painful that really is." The angel looked down at the lamb nestled peacefully in his arms.

"God hates death," the angel continued. "But He wants you to offer a sacrifice every time you sin. Perhaps," he sighed, "when you see how much it costs, you won't be tempted to sin so much."

Now it was Adam's turn to cry, but he knew he needed to obey.

"God knows best," he told Eve. "If we had trusted Him enough to obey in the first place, we wouldn't have to do this now."

Slowly they walked toward the Garden of Eden. They couldn't go inside, but they could worship God there at the gate. Eve waited while Adam built an altar. She watched while he lifted the little lamb up, laying it gently on top of the altar. Then Adam's broad shoulders shook with sobs as he raised his hand to kill the little lamb. Thinking she could not stand to see any more, she covered her eyes with her hands. At that moment an angel hand rested tenderly on her shoulder.

"Look, Eve," the angel said gently. "You must look, or you won't understand."

And so she did. It was the hardest thing she had ever done, but as she looked, she started to understand. And she gave her heart to Jesus that day in a deeper and fuller way than she had ever done before. Because when she realized how much Jesus loved her, what He was willing to do for her, she wanted to love Him right back.

Of course, Adam was having many of the same feelings himself. Great tears ran down his cheeks, for here he was, raising his hand to take a life that only God could give. It was the first time Adam had killed anything himself. In his heart, he knew that such a thing would never have happened if he had only obeyed God. What made it even worse, of course, was to think that not only this lamb, but the Son of God must someday also die for his sins.

FAMILY BIBLE STORY
SERIES

O
ne of the most extensively researched Bible story books on the market today, this series offers features which give background information to engage every member of the family, young and old alike. Written by Ruth Redding Brand and illustrated by distinguished artists, these carefully researched and beautifully illustrated books will make Bible characters come alive for your children. Every name, place, and custom is carefully explained. Hardcover. Available individually or as a set.

Abraham, 109 pages. ISBN 0-8280-1856-1
Adam & Eve, 95 pages. ISBN 0-8280-1850-2
Jacob, 127 pages. ISBN 0-8280-1852-9
Joseph, 87 pages. ISBN 0-8280-1854-5

Quick order online at www.AdventistBookCenter.com
Call 1-800-765-6955
Visit your local Adventist Book Center®
Or ask for it wherever books are sold

REVIEW AND HERALD®
PUBLISHING ASSOCIATION